PARIS FASHIONS

Racehorse for Young Readers books may be purchased in bulk at special discounts for sales promotion, corporate gifts, fund-raising, or educational purposes. Special editions can also be created to specifications. For details, contact the Special Sales Department, Skyhorse Publishing, 307 West 36th Street, 11th Floor, New York, NY 10018 or info@skyhorsepublishing.com.

Racehorse for Young Readers™ is a pending trademark of Skyhorse Publishing, Inc.®, a Delaware corporation.

Visit our website at www.skyhorsepublishing.com.

10 9 8 7 6 5 4 3 2

Cover and interior artwork credit: Karma Voce

Print ISBN: 978-1-944686-60-4

Printed in the United States of America

Forever Inspired COLORING BOOK

PARIS FASHIONS

KARMA VOCE

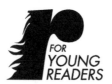

FOR YOUNG READERS

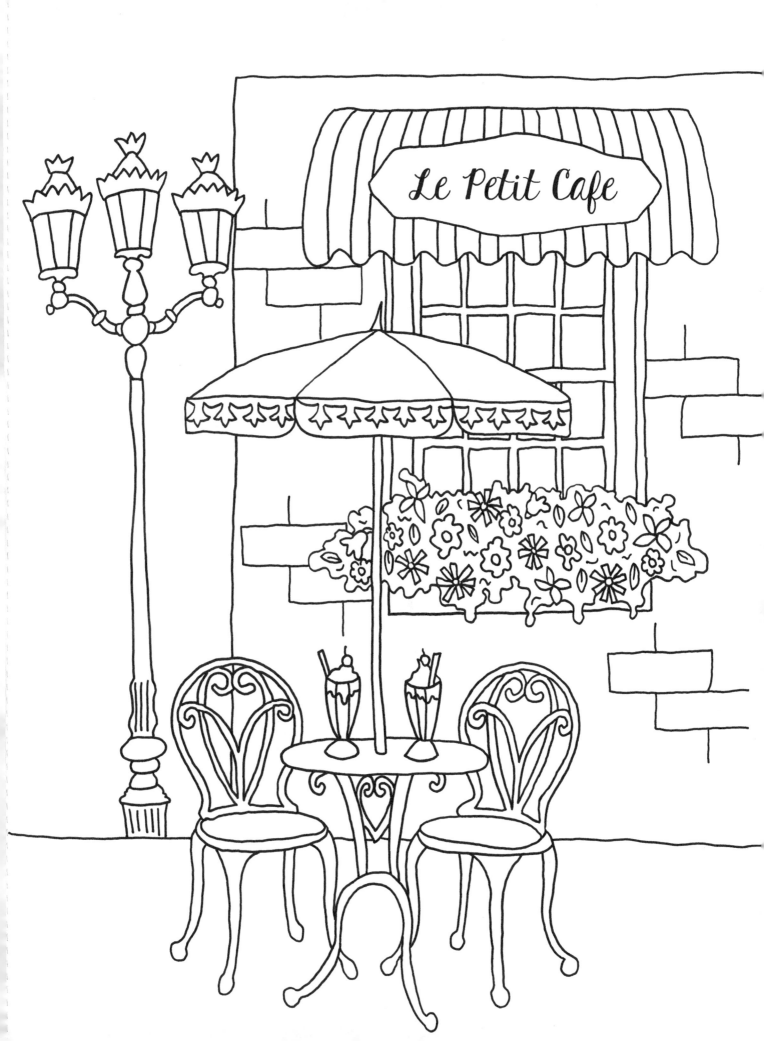

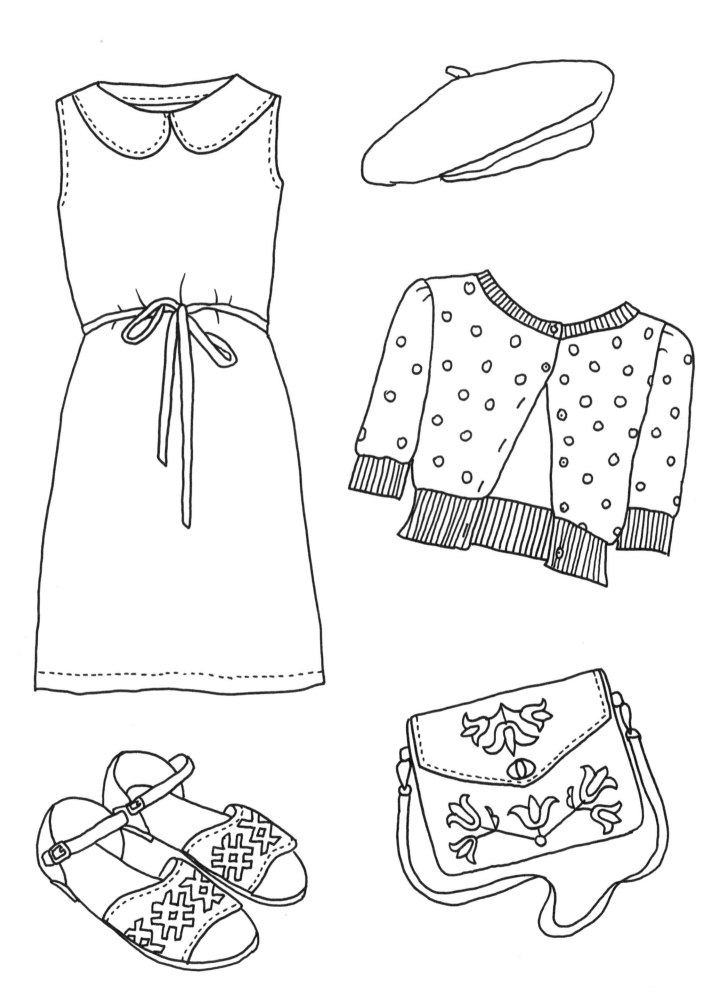

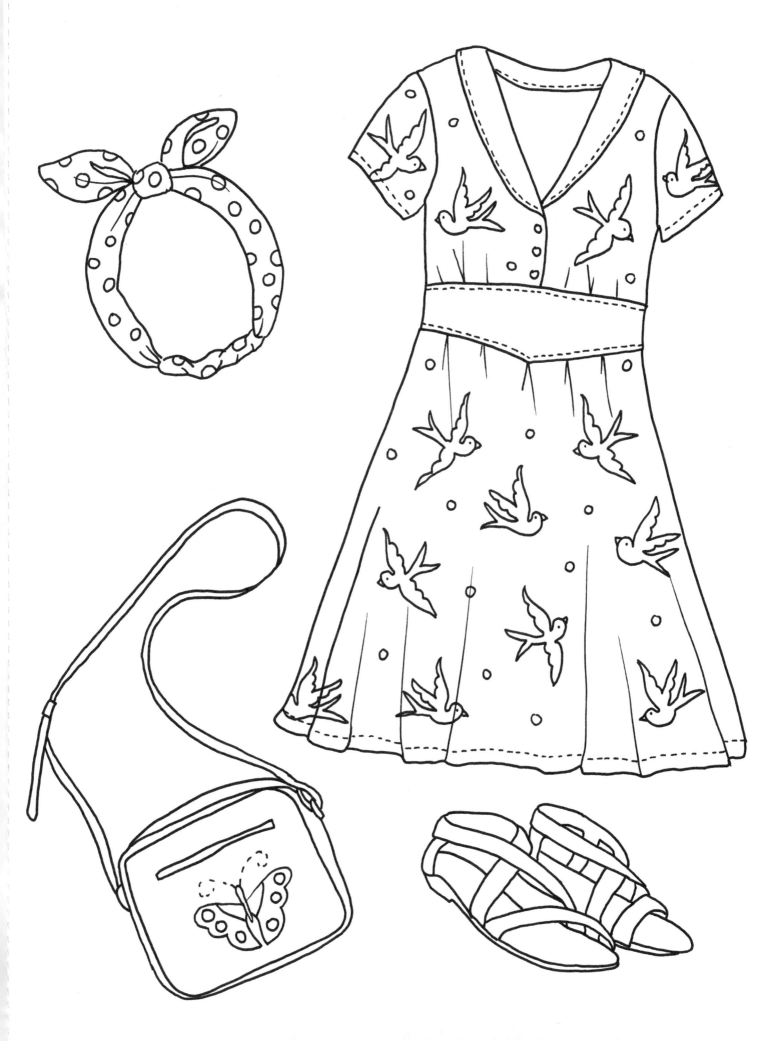

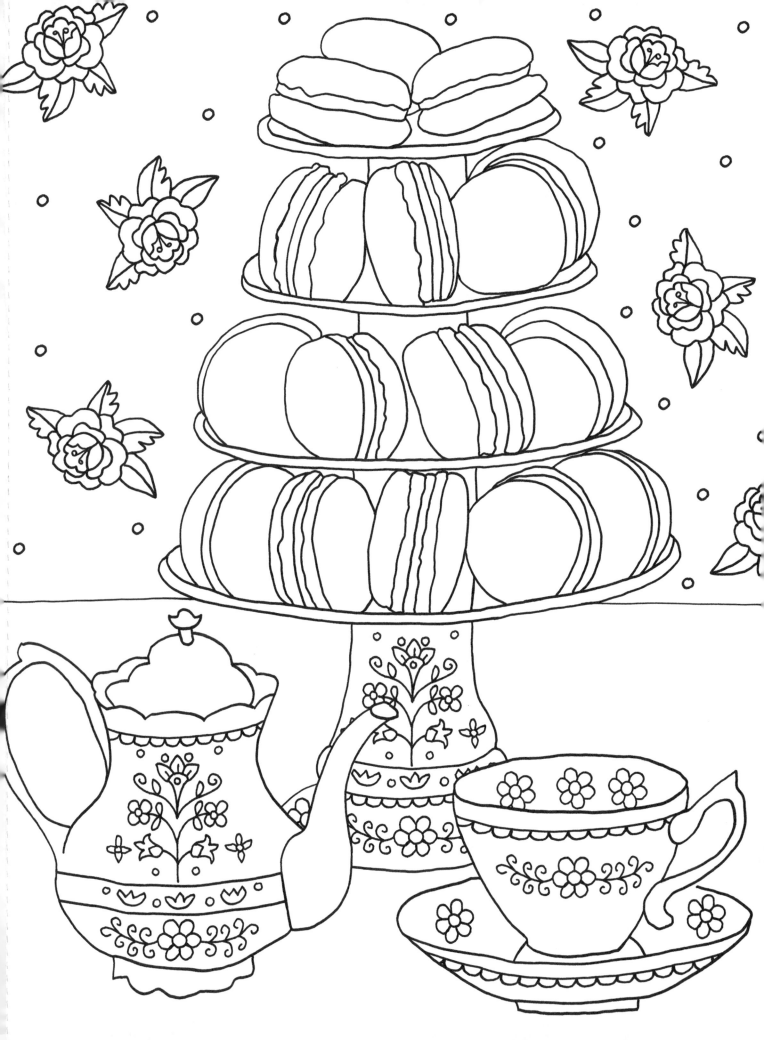

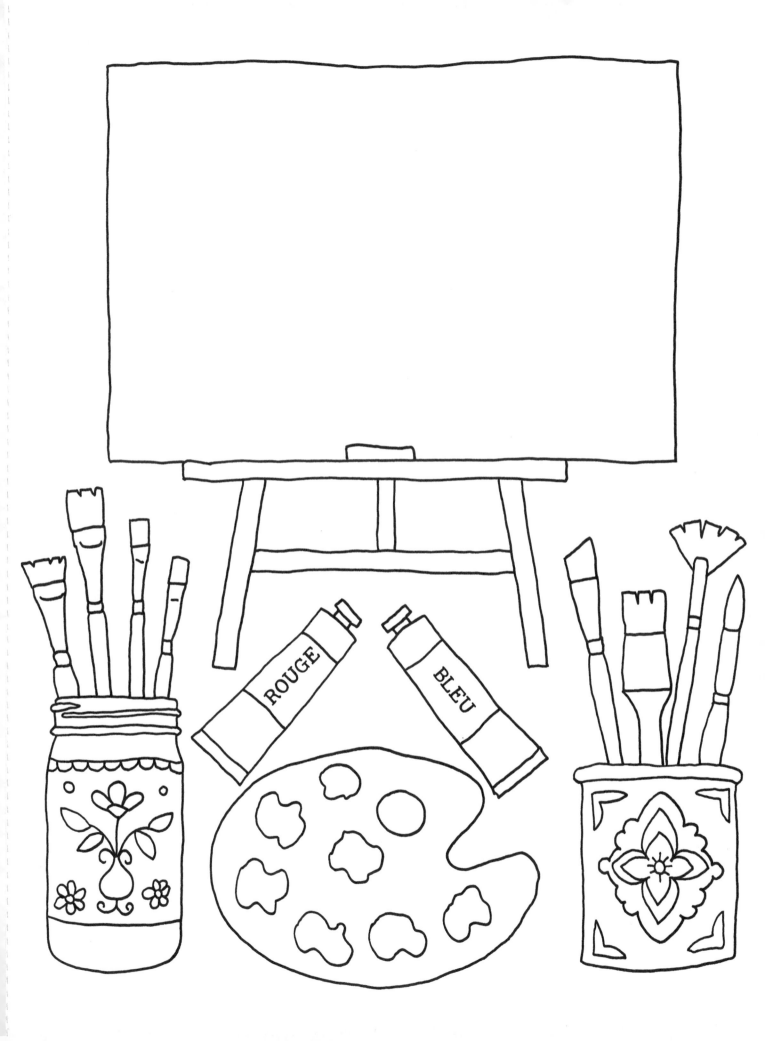

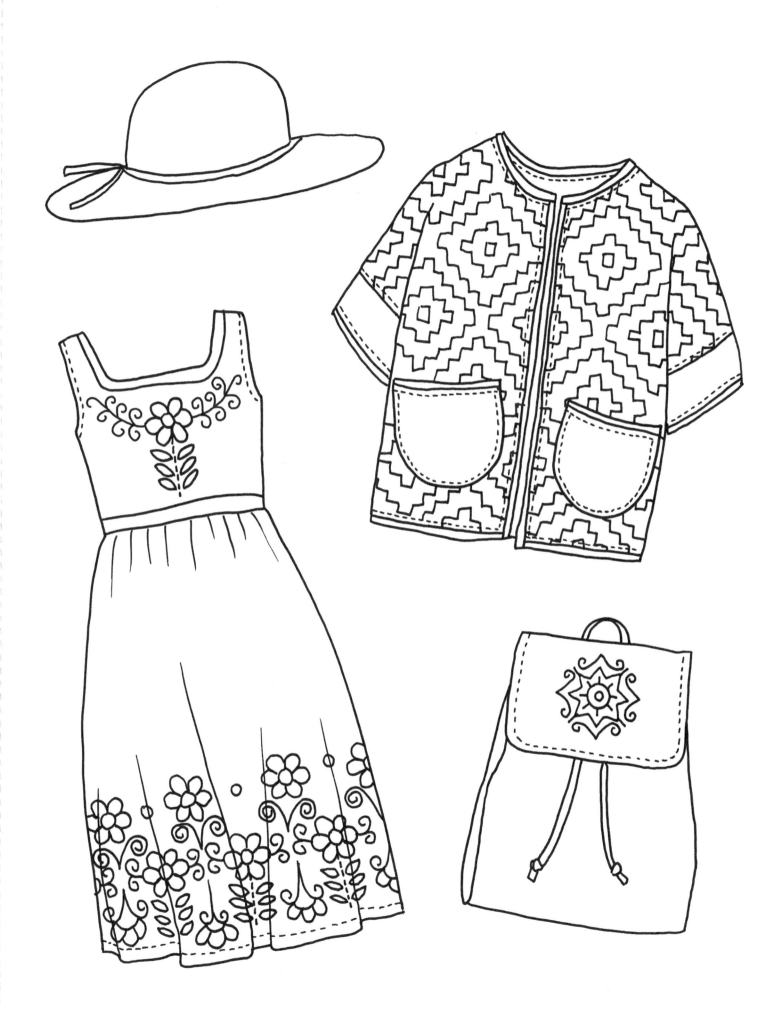

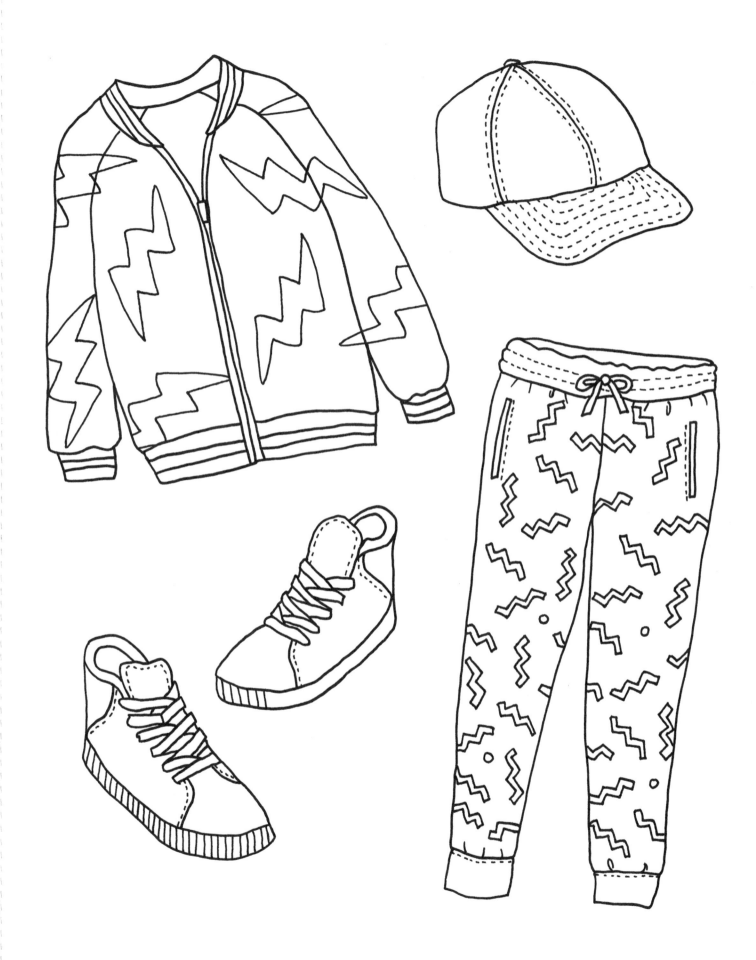

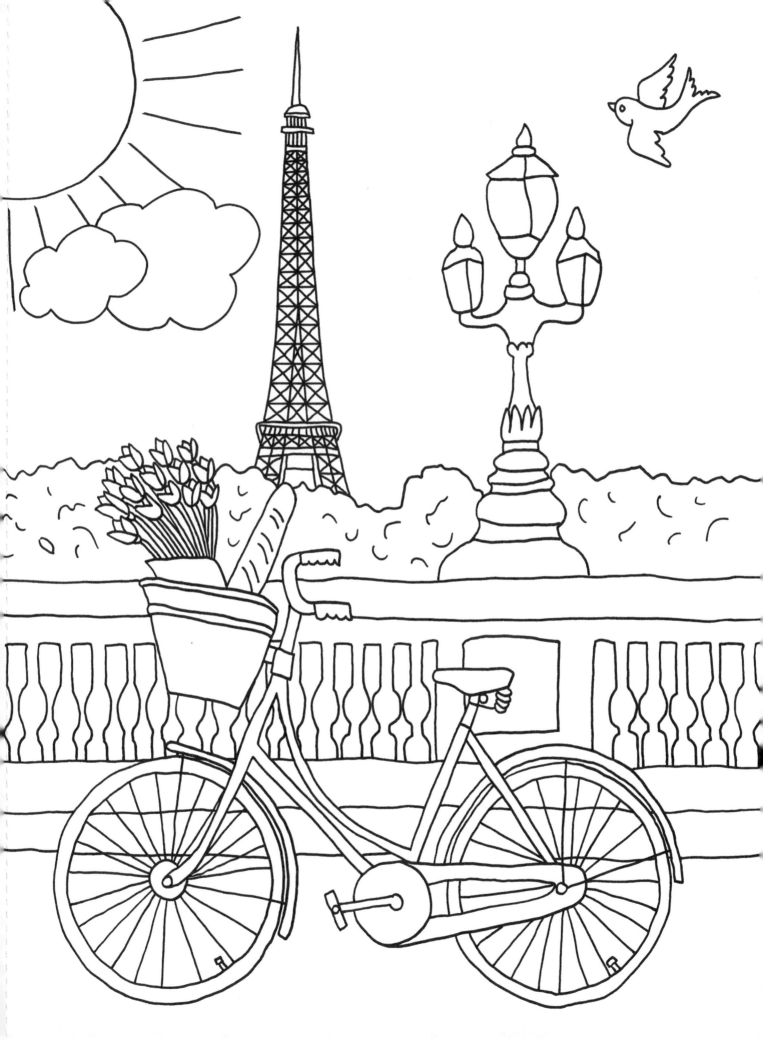

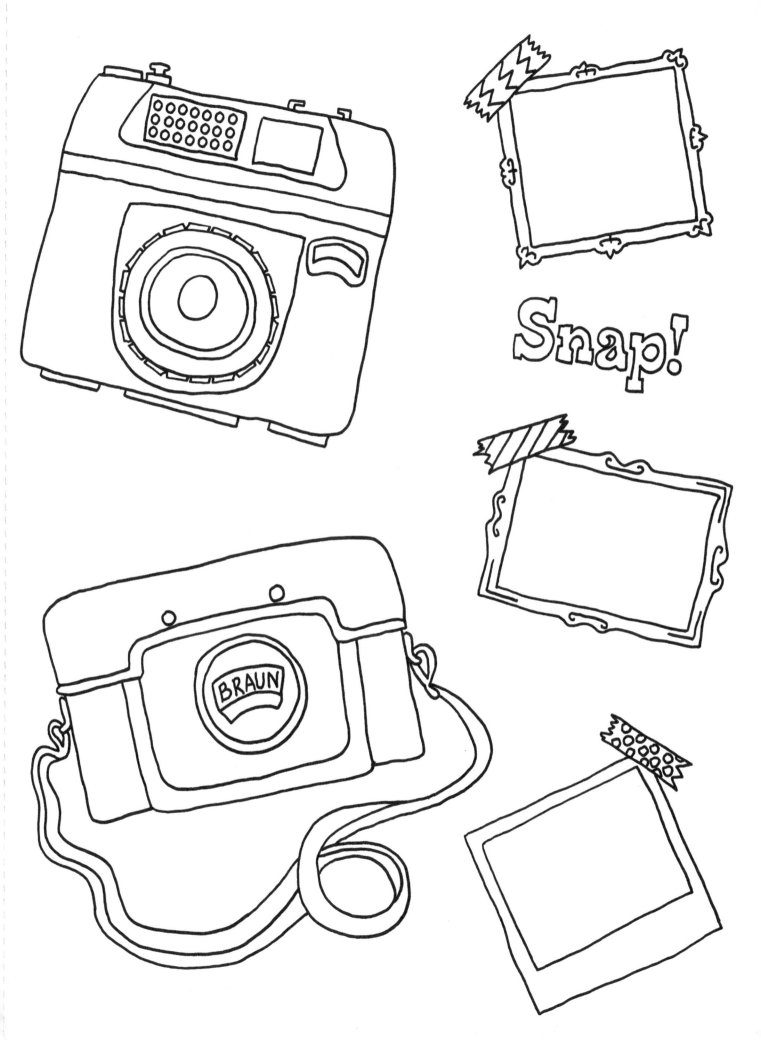

Snap!

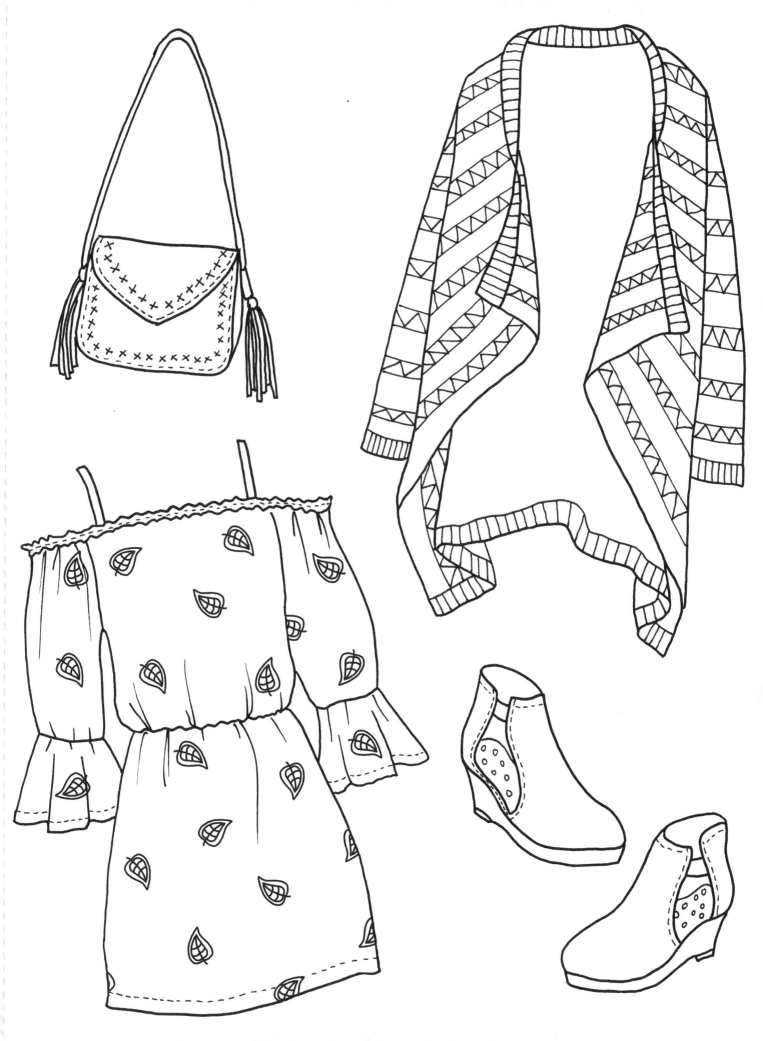

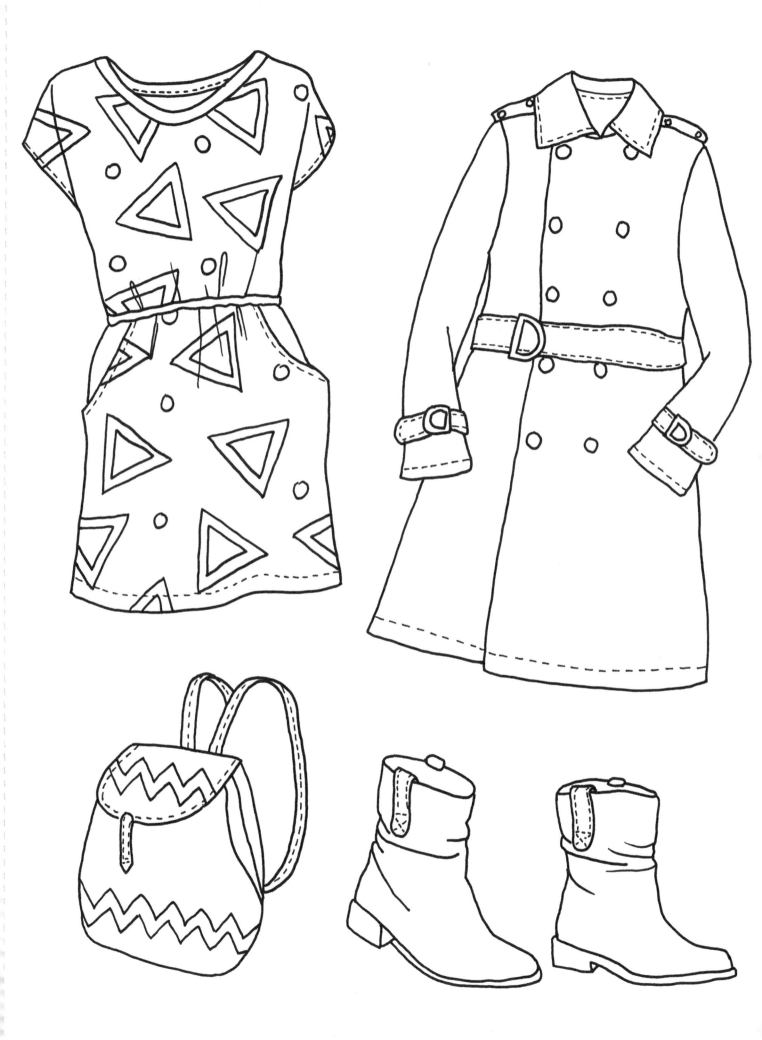

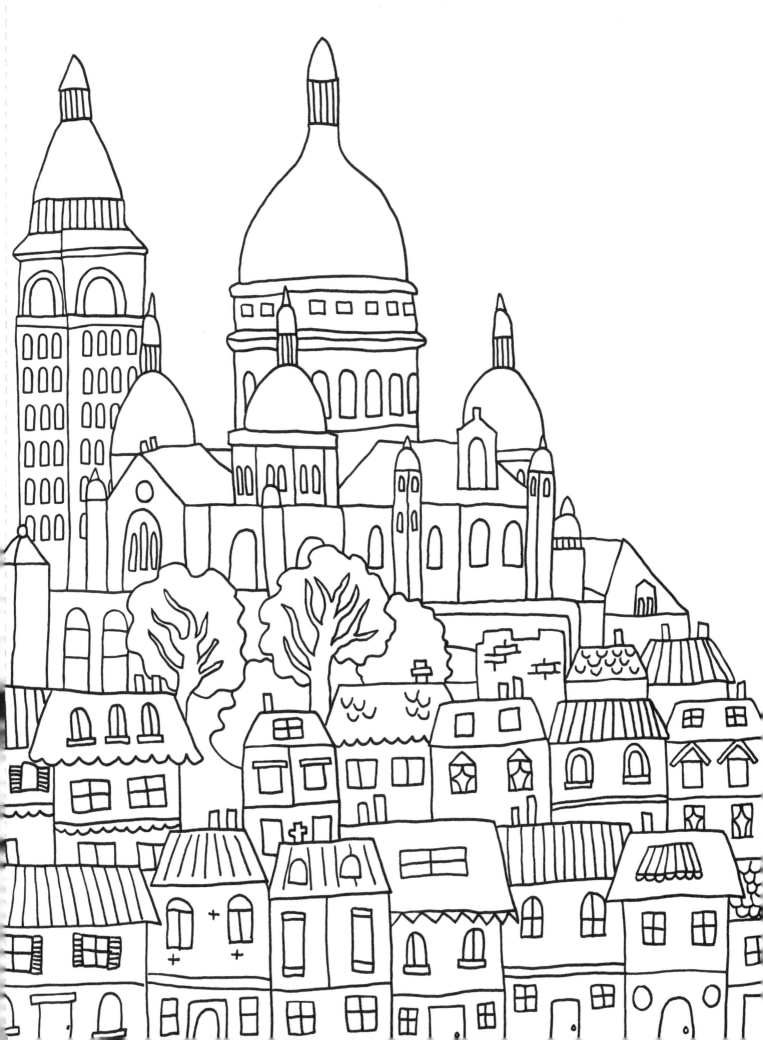

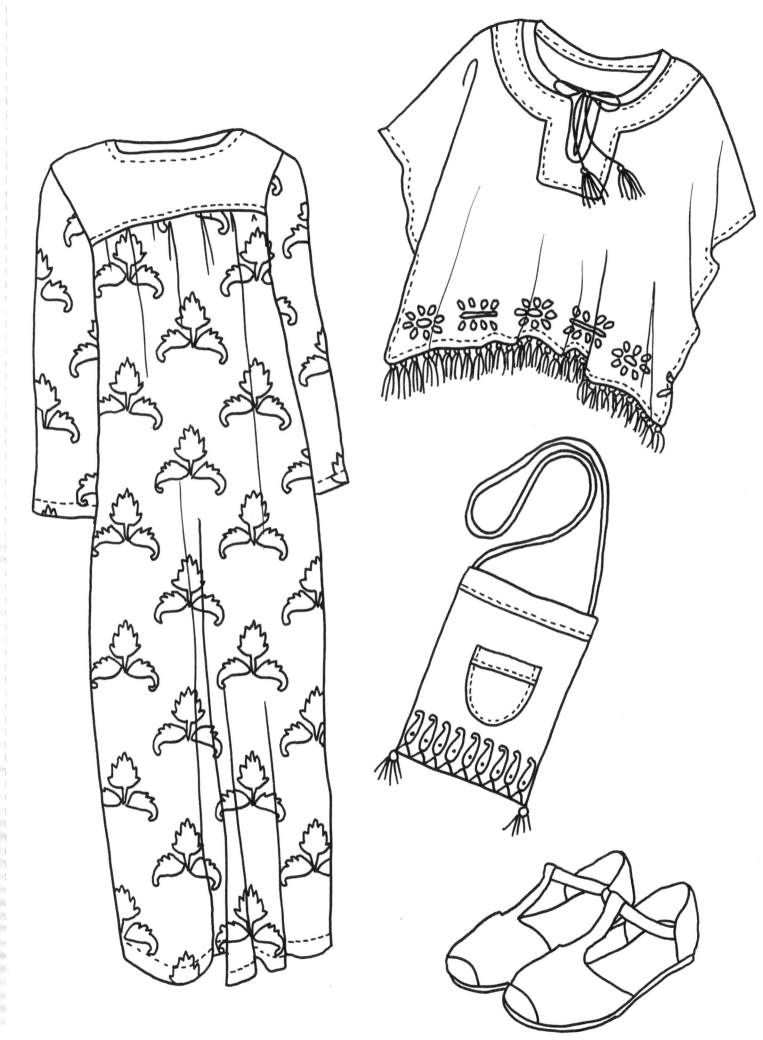

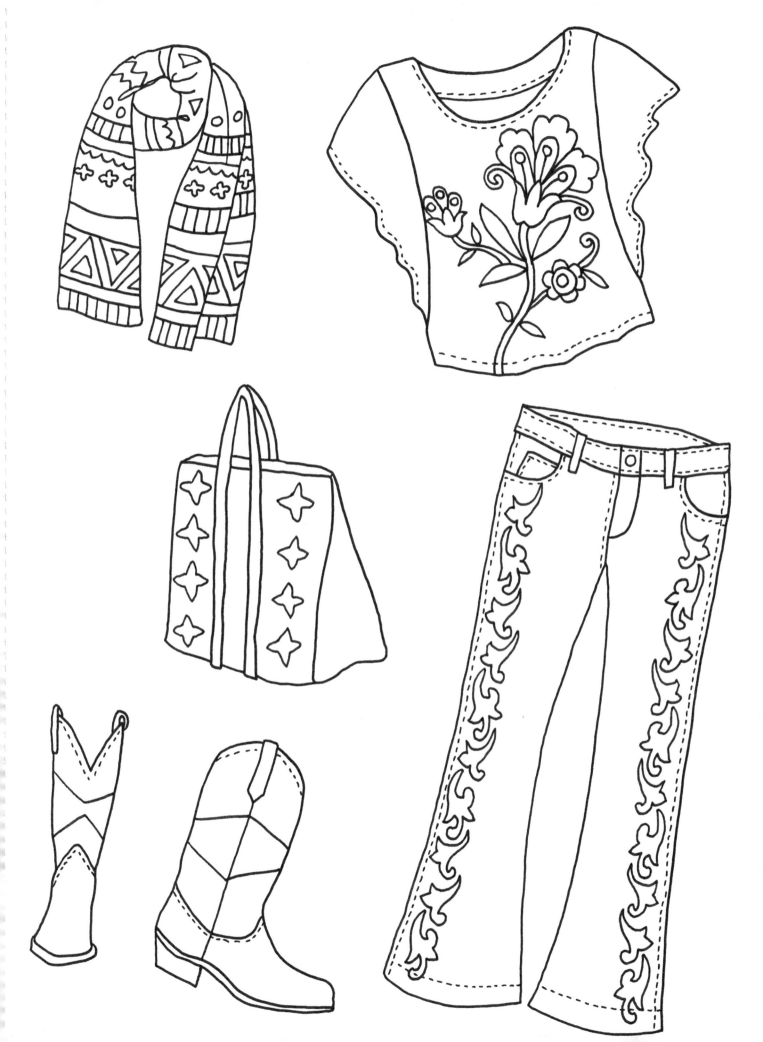

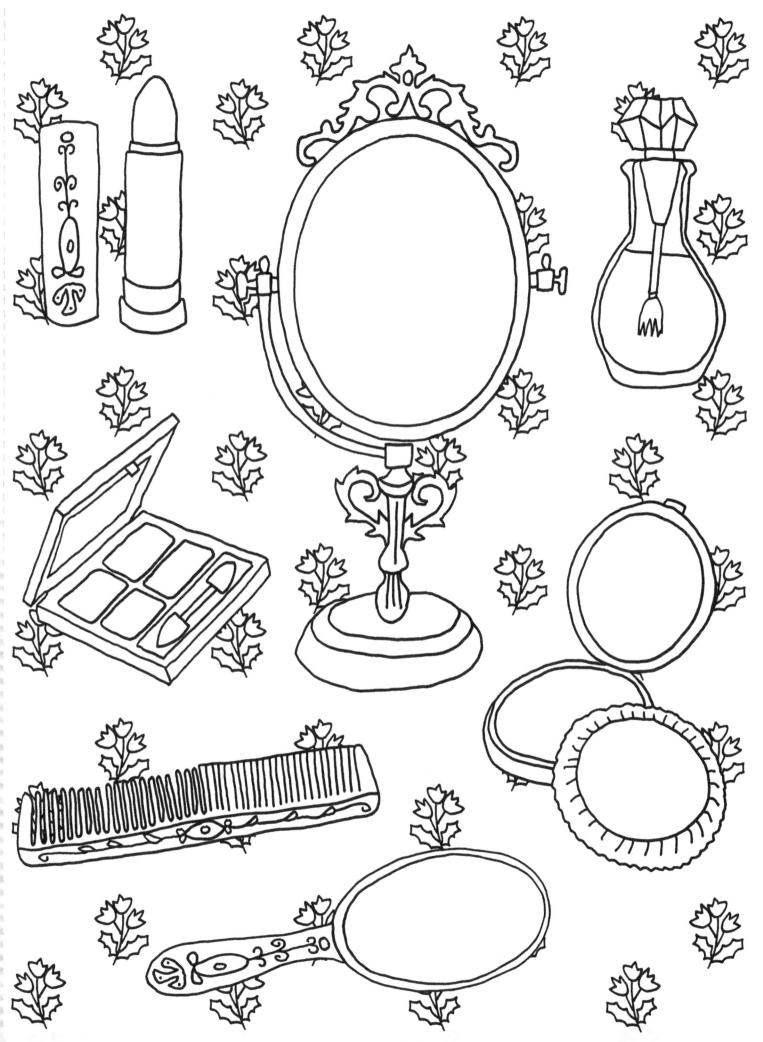

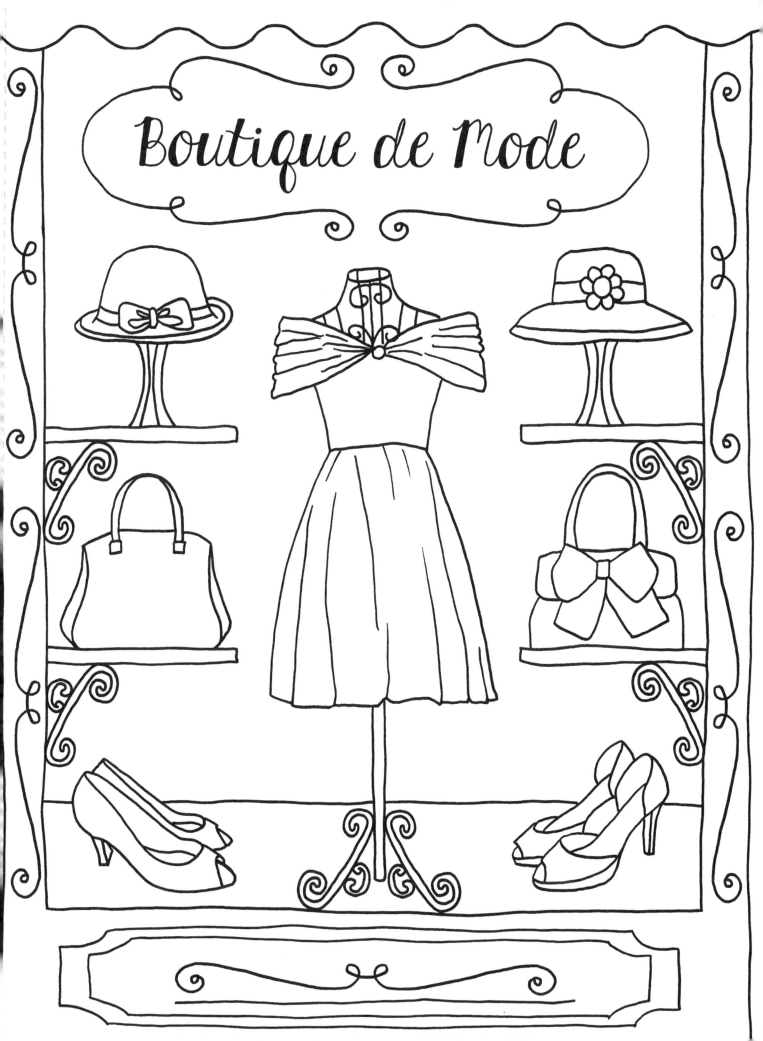

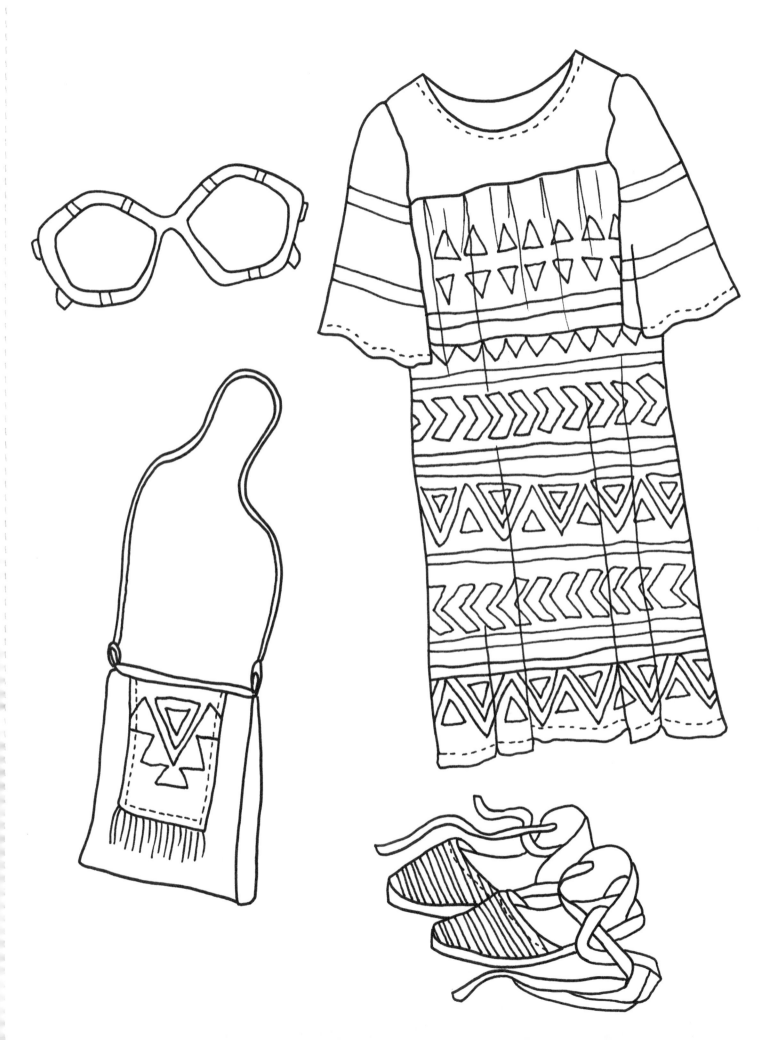

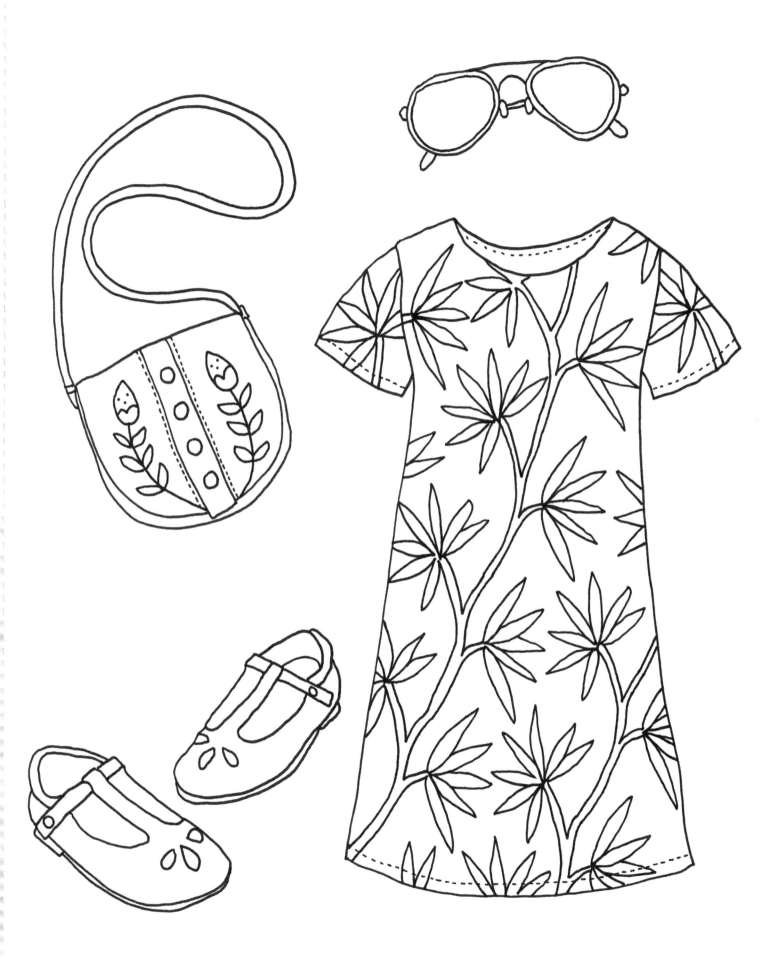

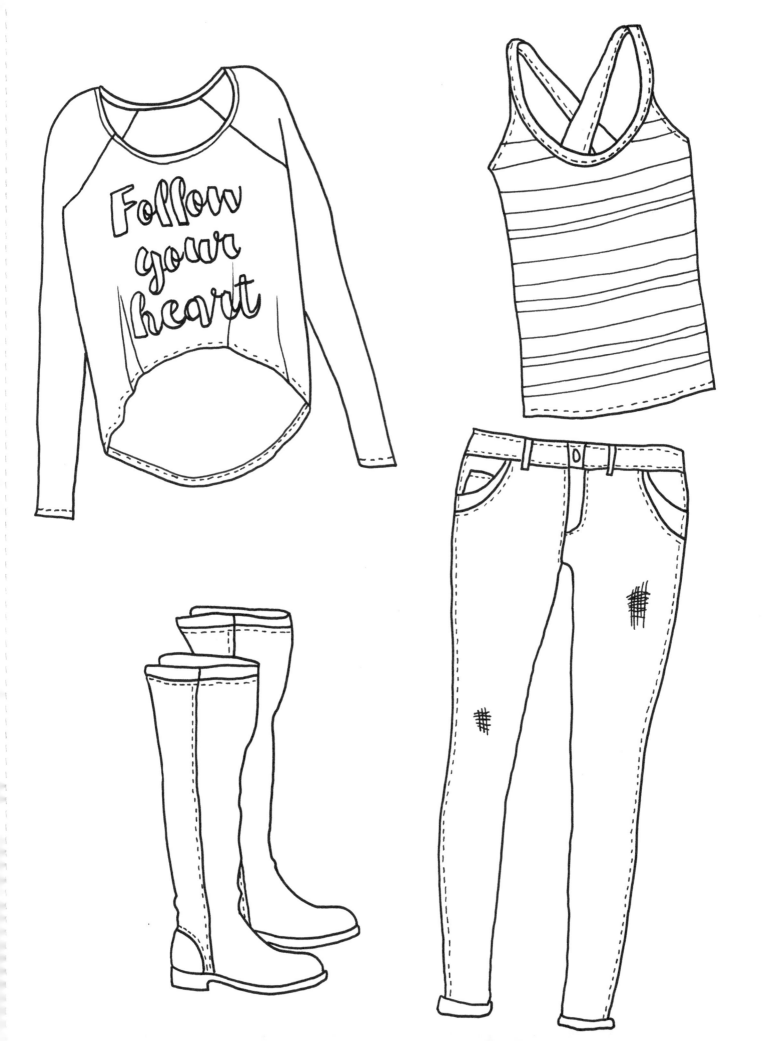

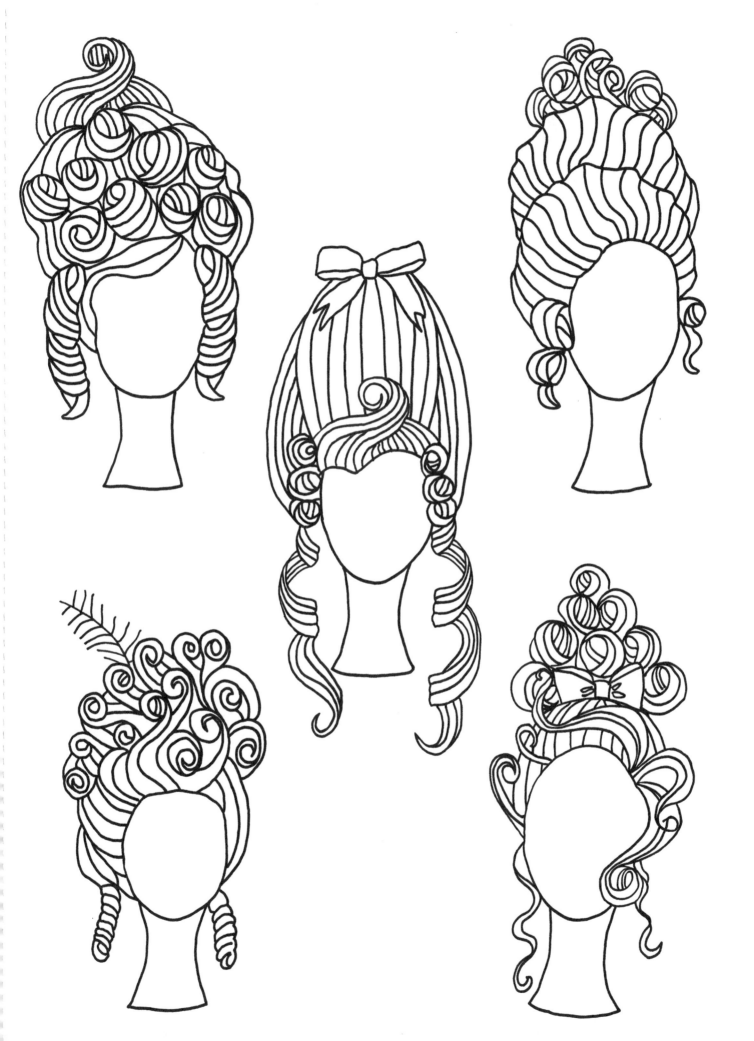

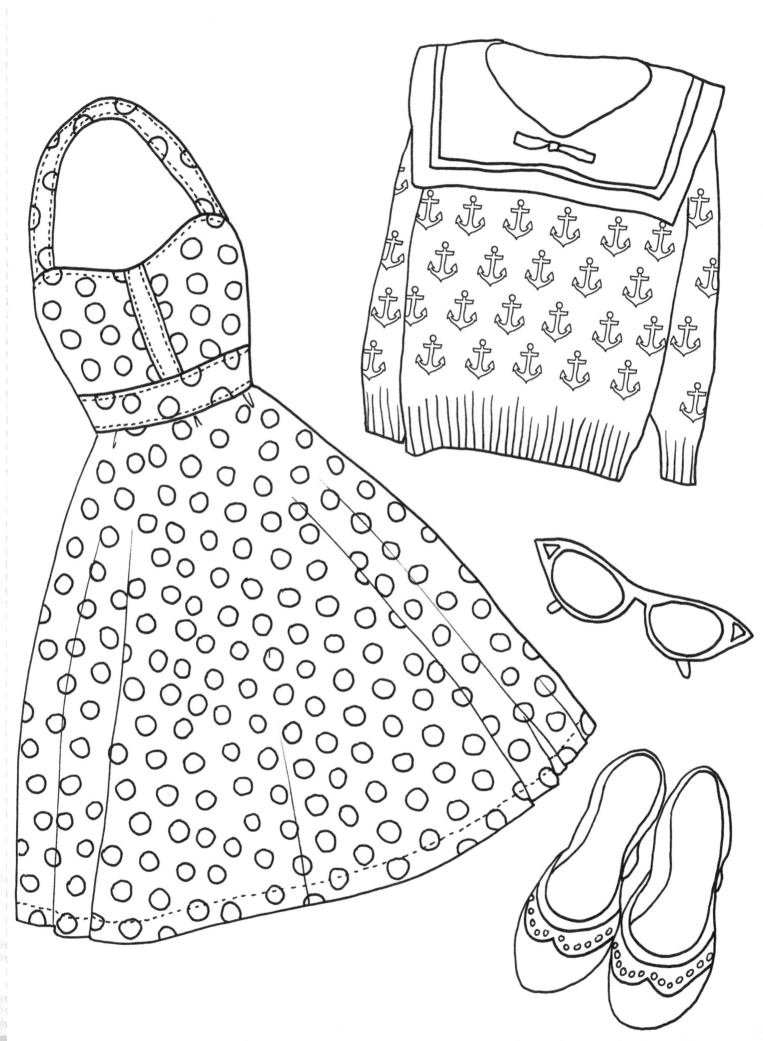

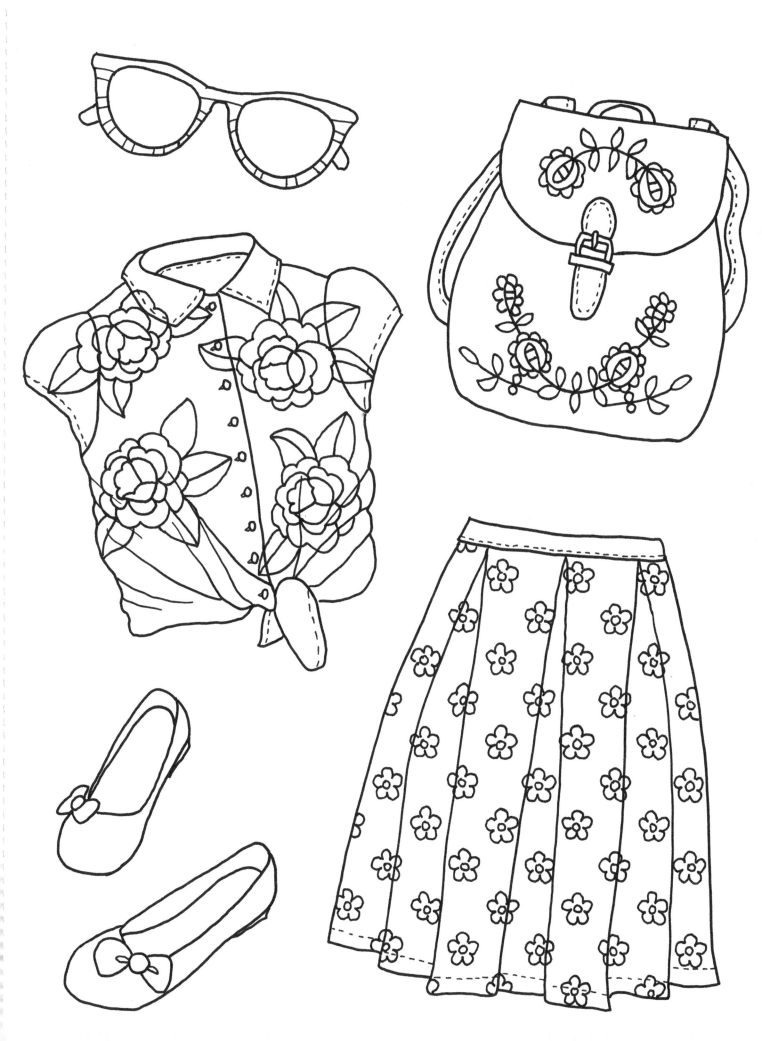

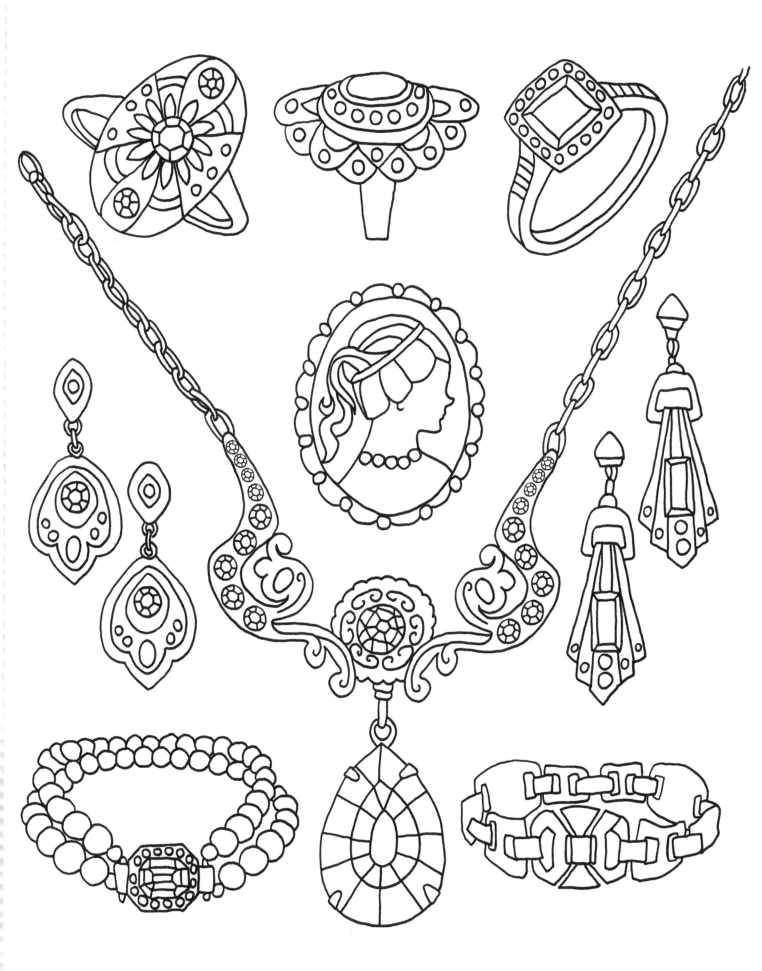

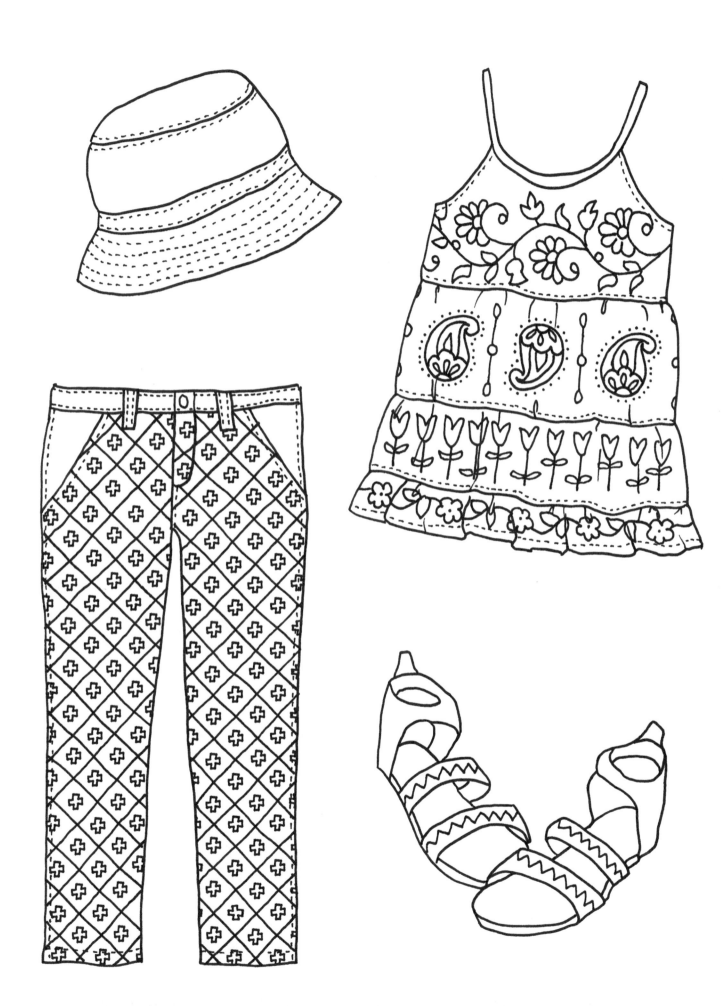

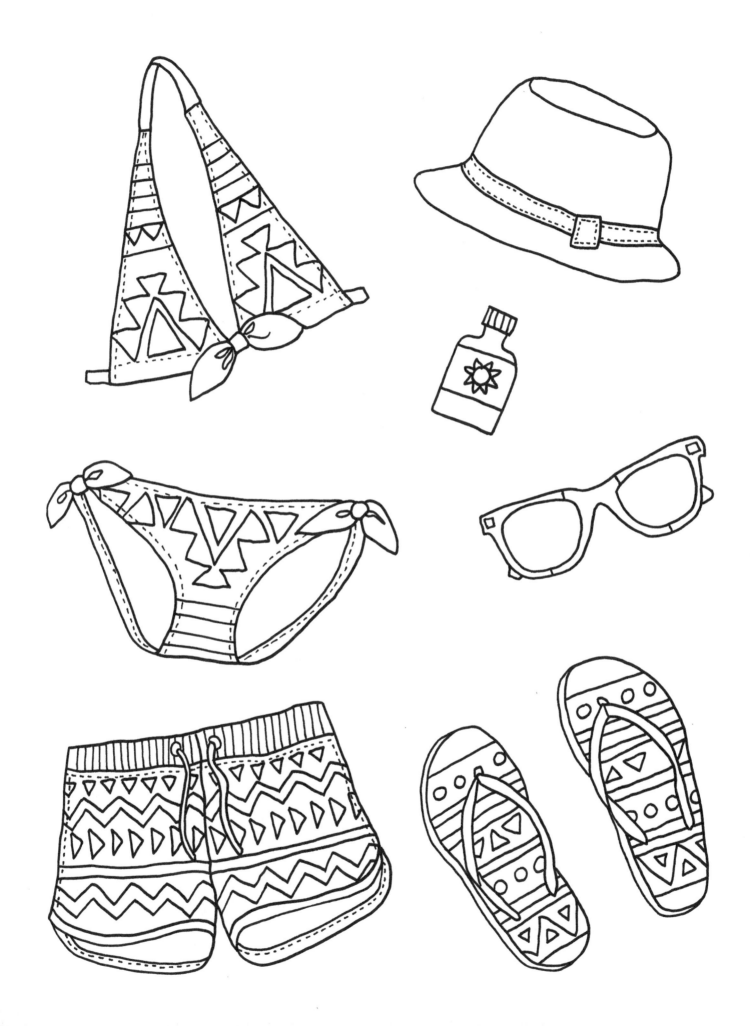

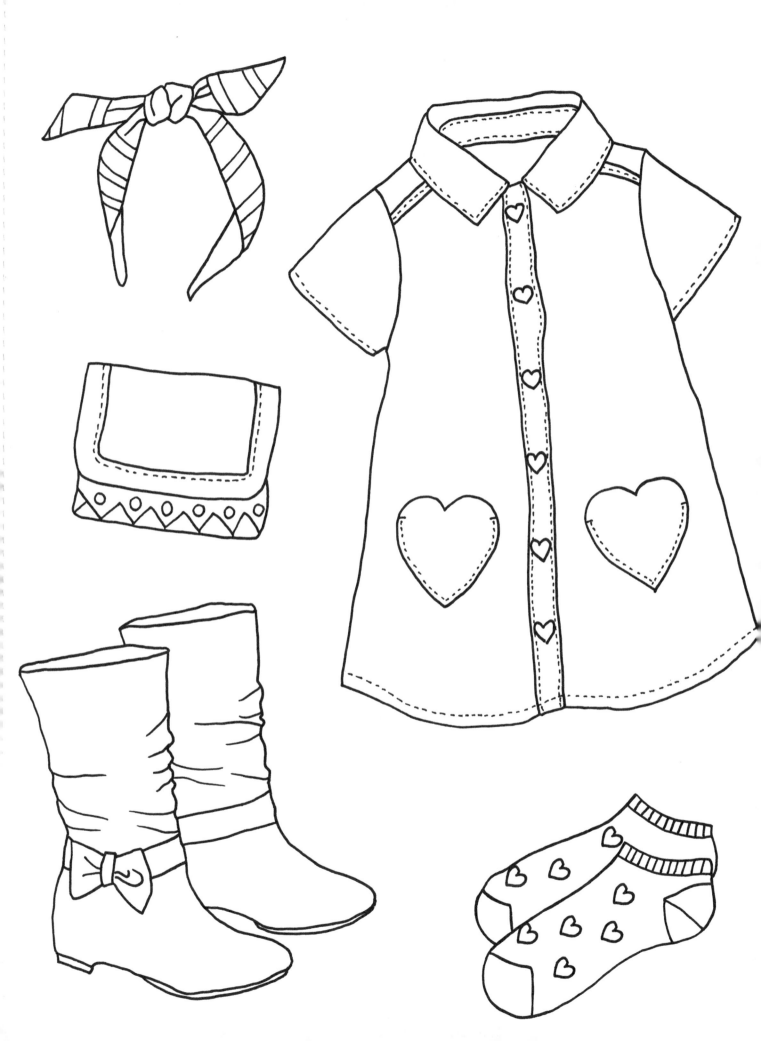

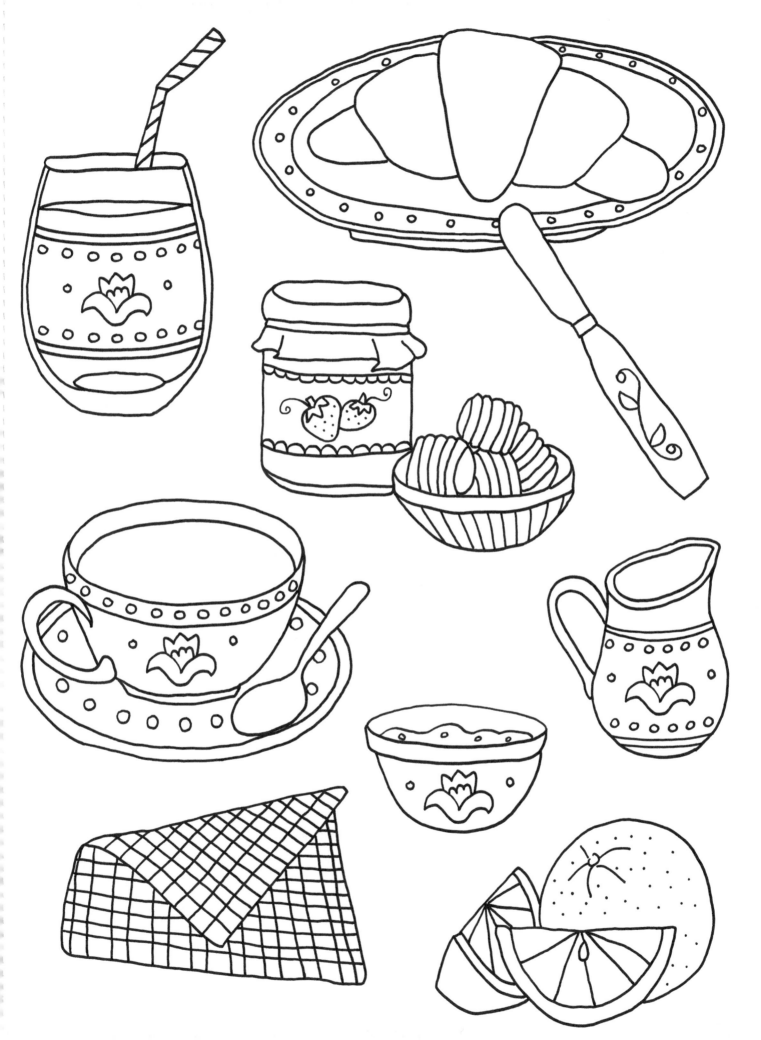

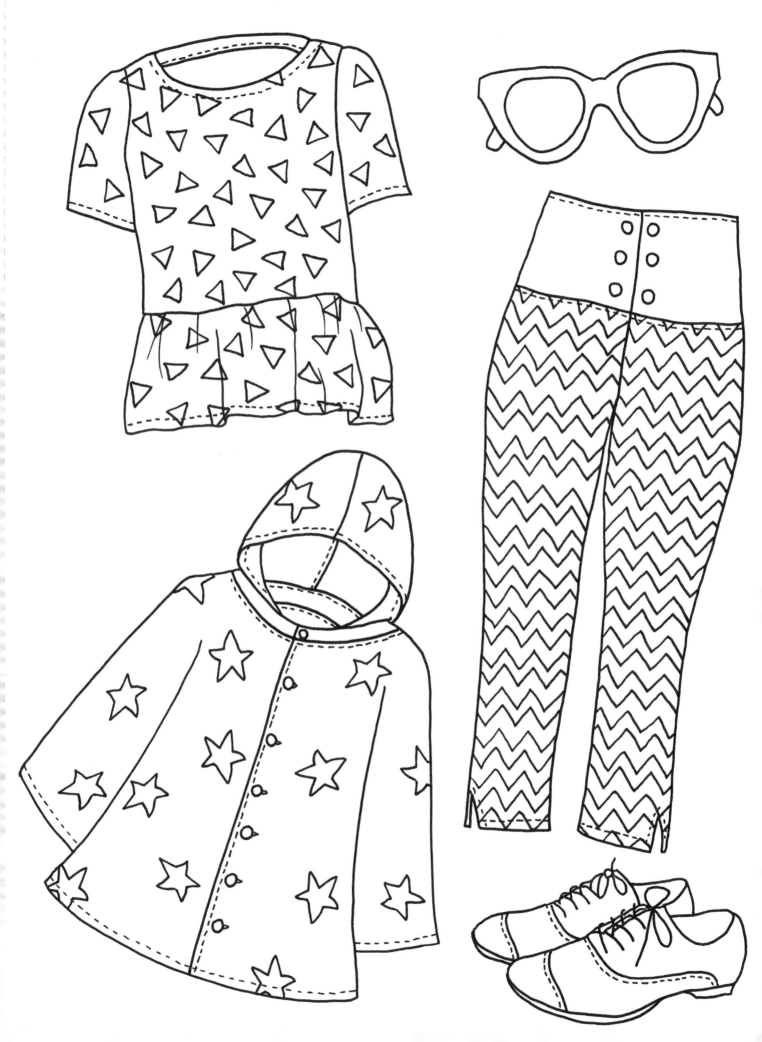

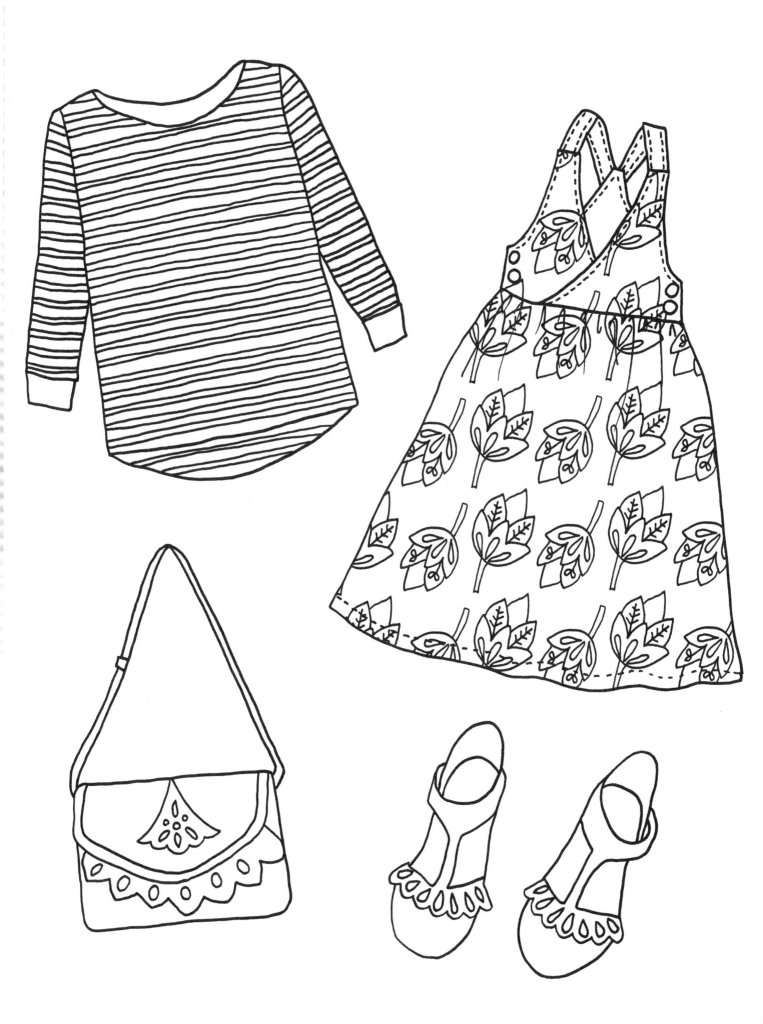

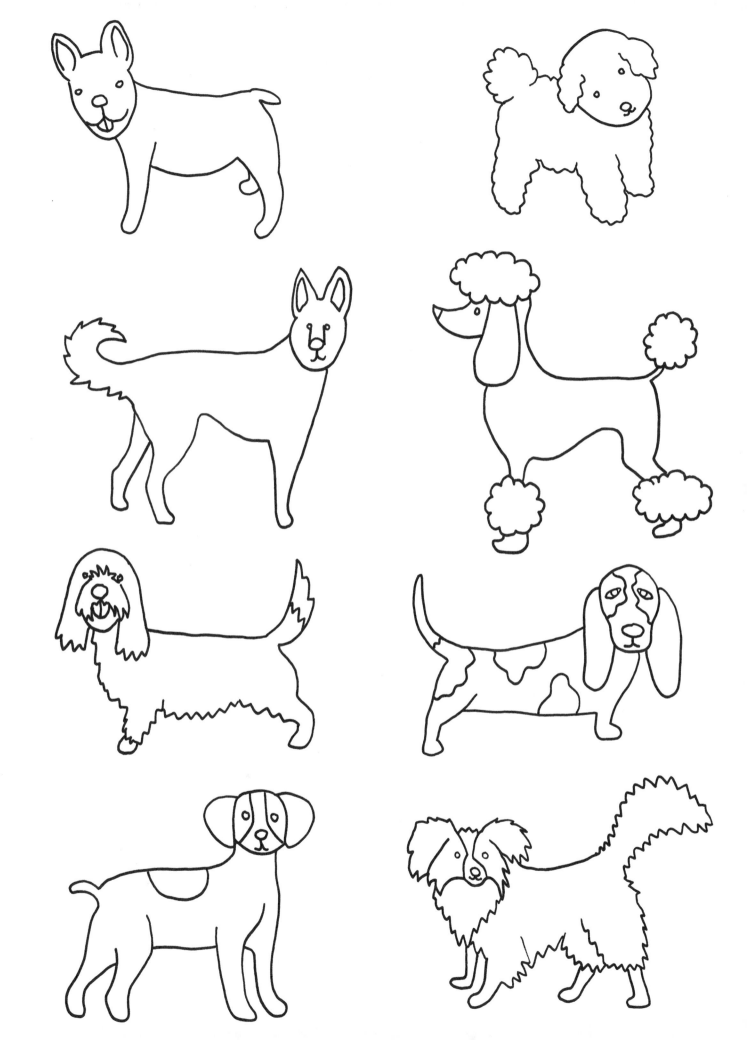

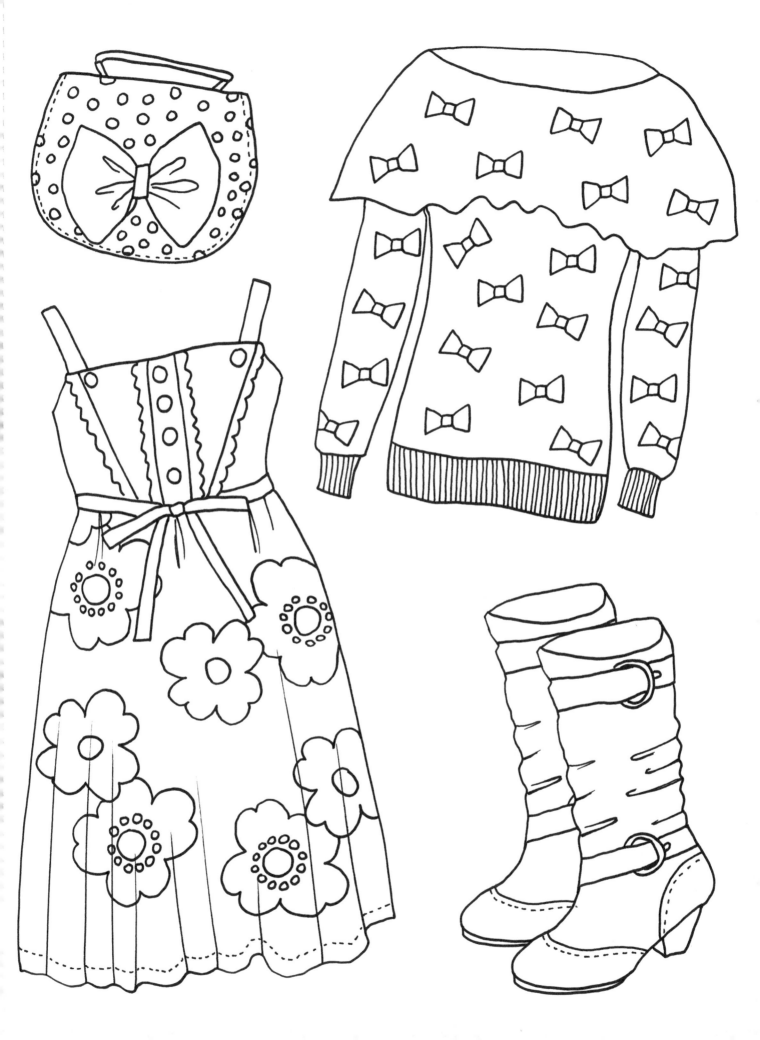

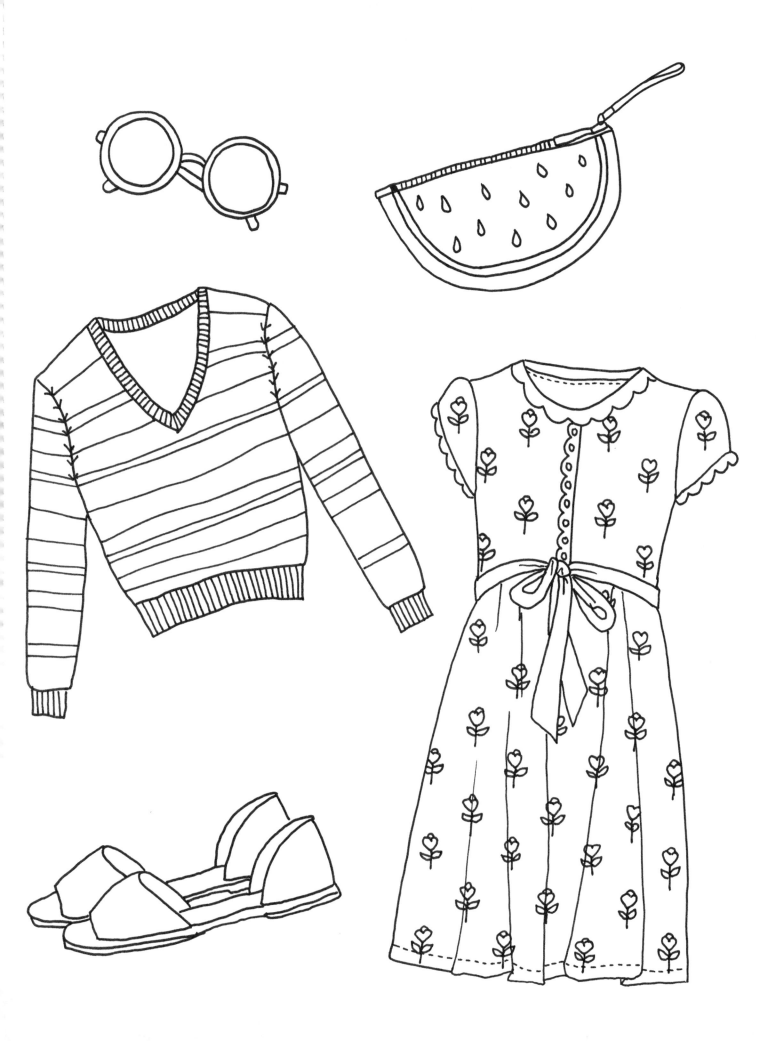

EAU DE
PARFUM

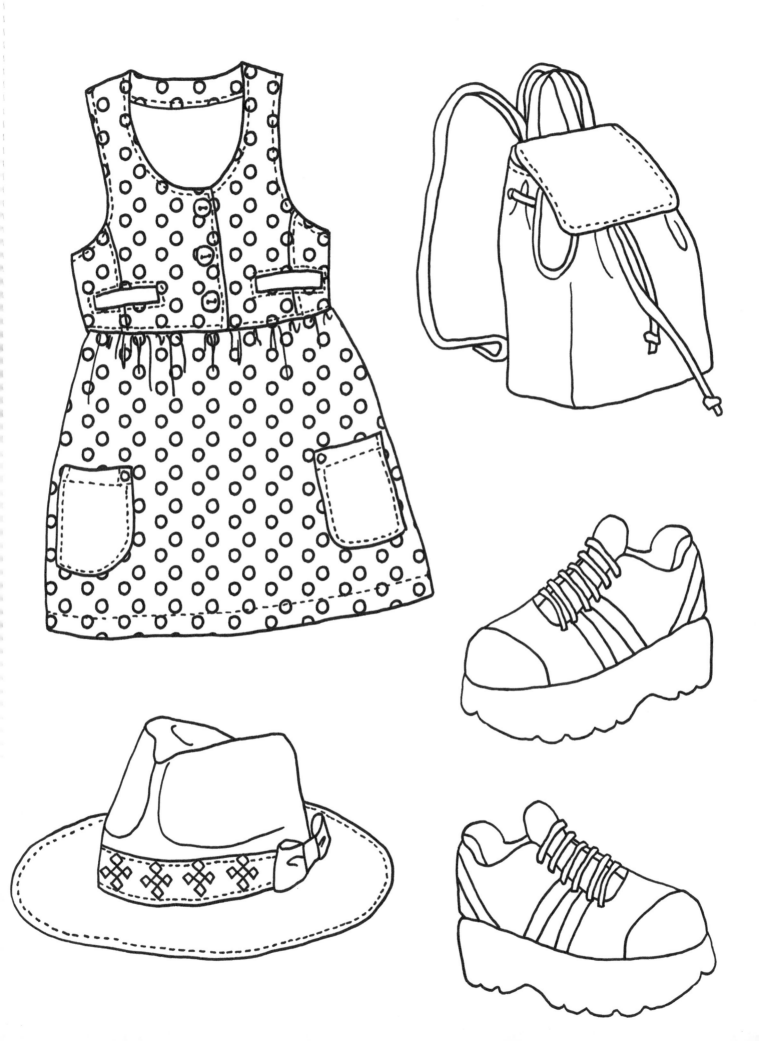

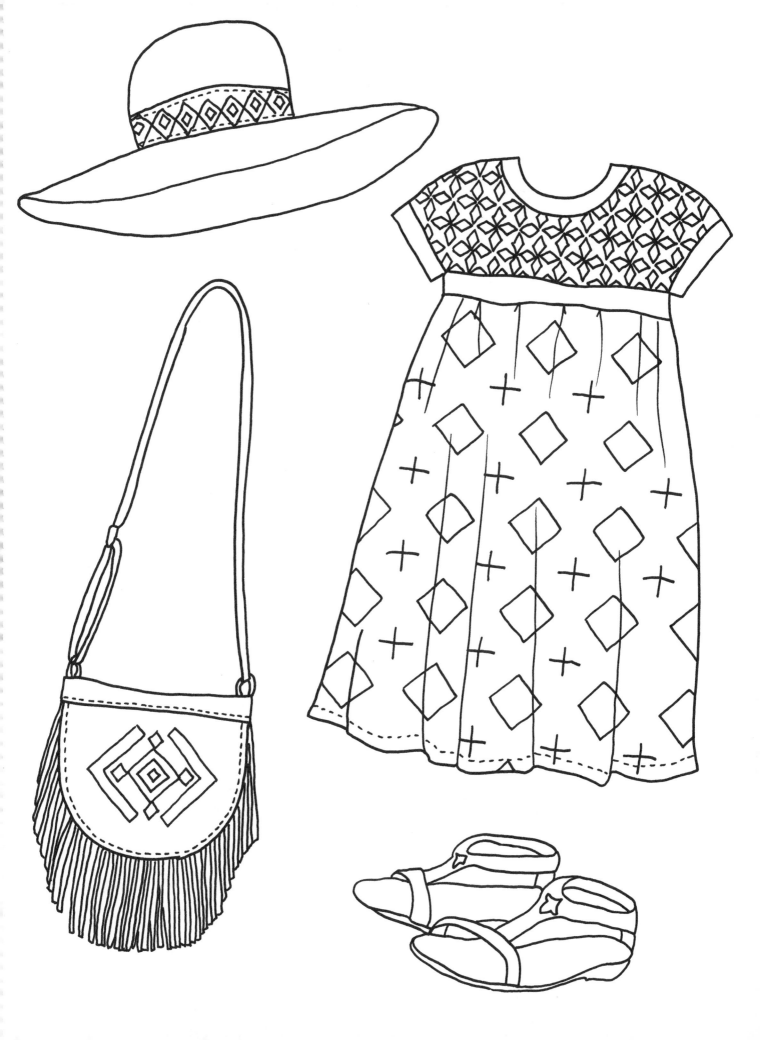

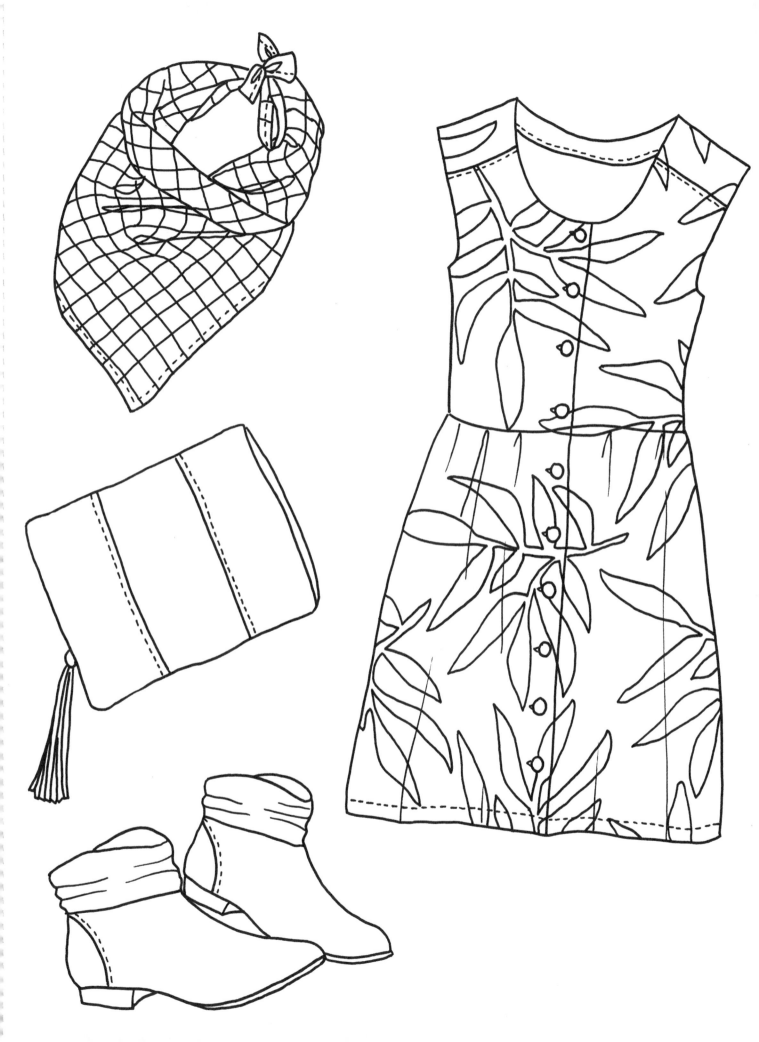

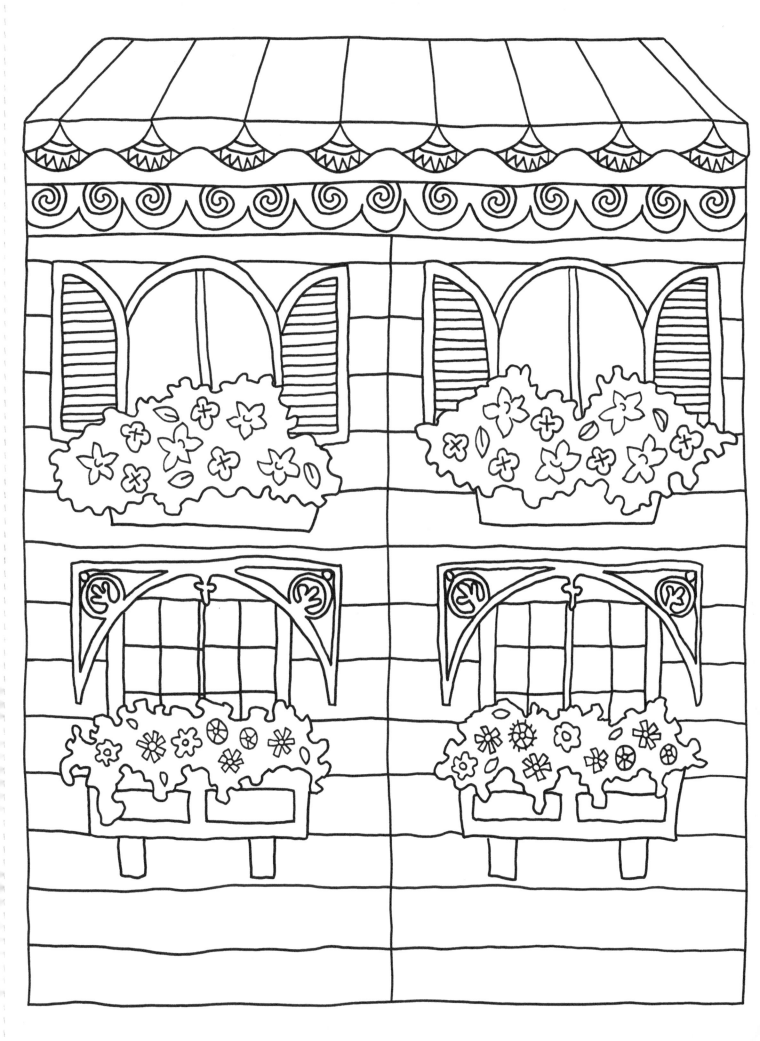

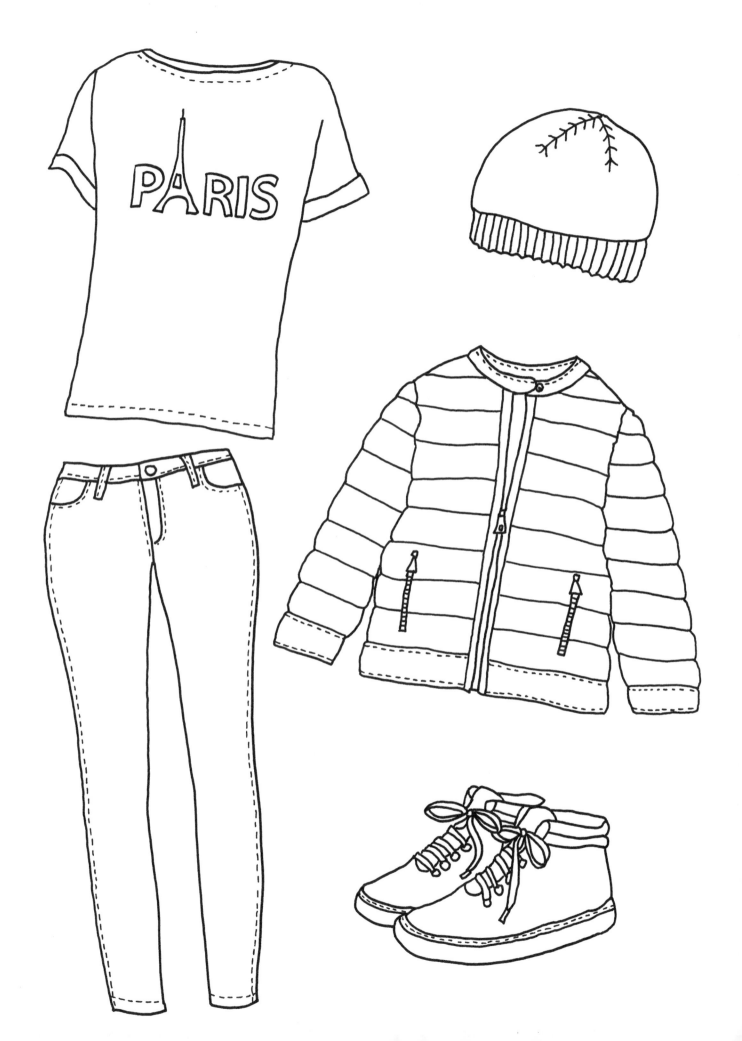

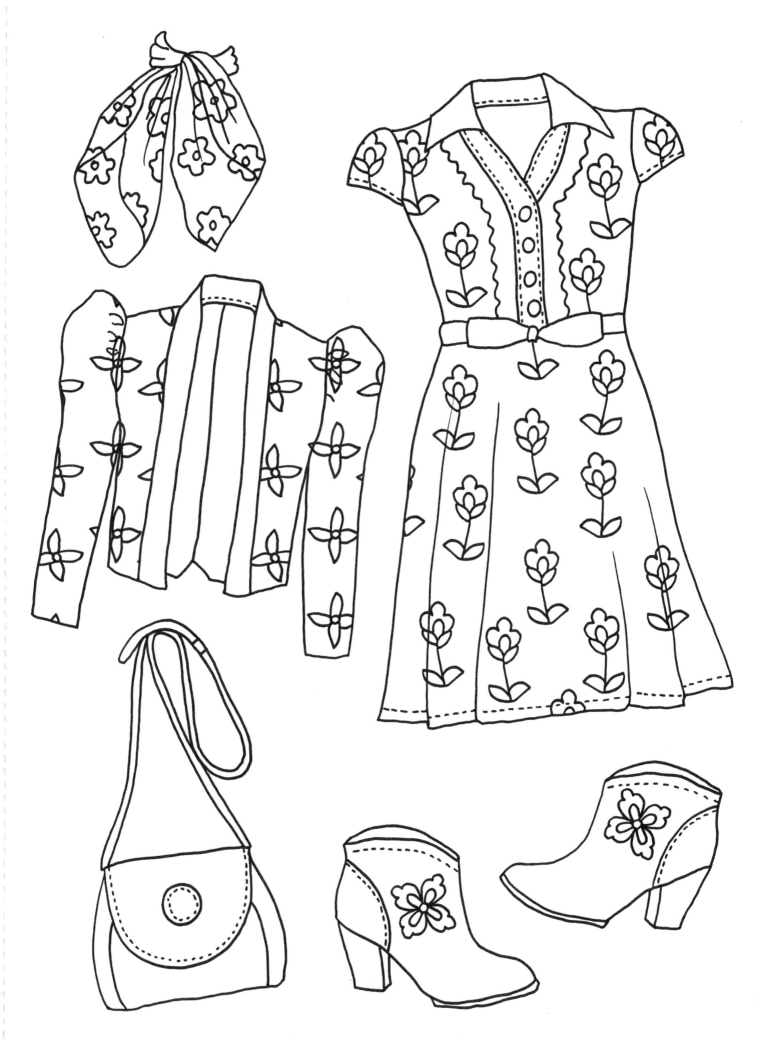

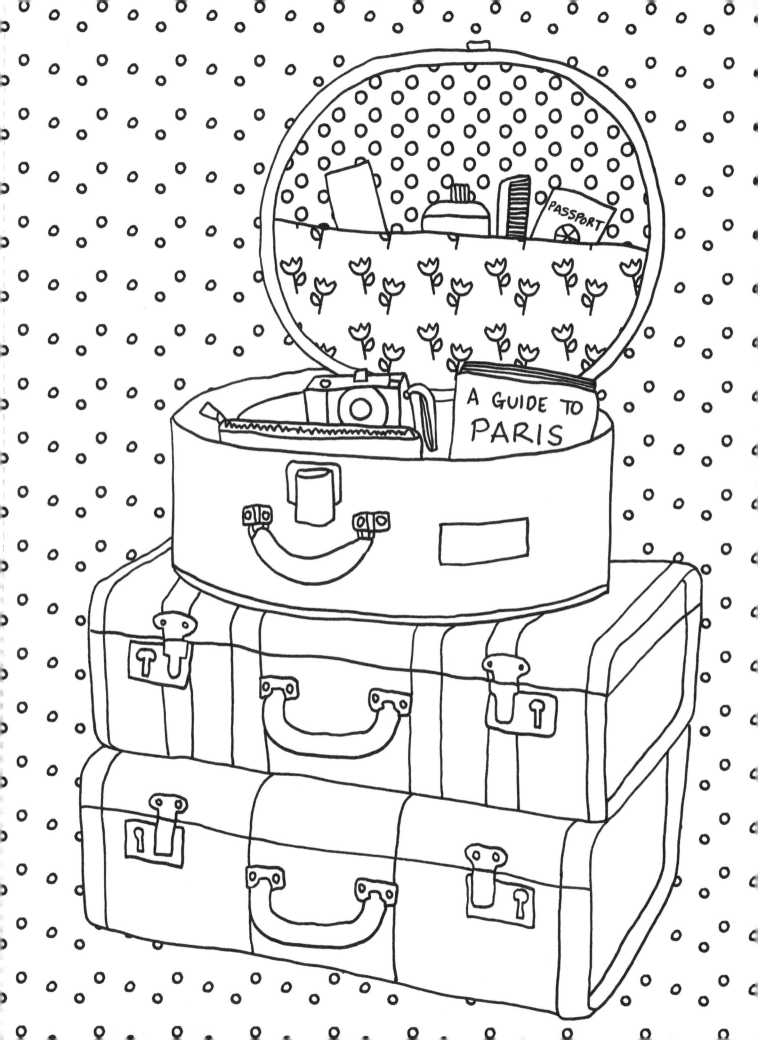

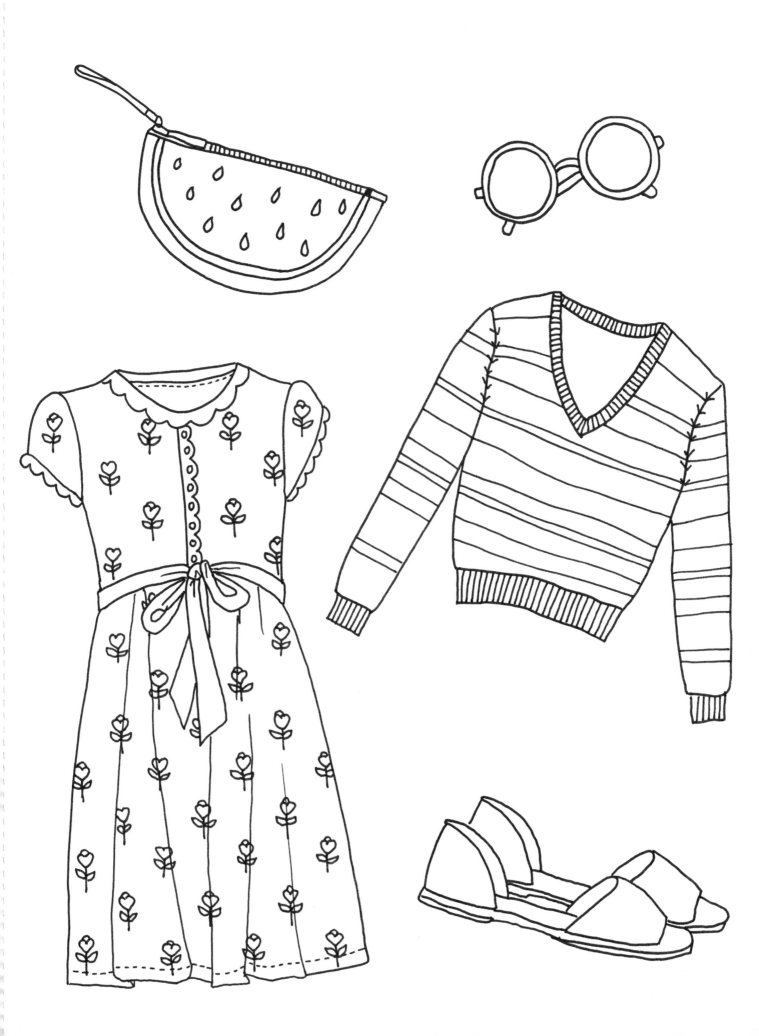

Color Bars

Use these bars to test your coloring medium and palette. Don't be afraid to try unique color combinations!

Color Bars

Use these bars to test your coloring medium and palette. Don't be afraid to try unique color combinations!

Color Bars

Use these bars to test your coloring medium and palette. Don't be afraid to try unique color combinations!

Color Bars

Use these bars to test your coloring medium and palette. Don't be afraid to try unique color combinations!